A Rainbow,
of Time
and of Space

A Rainbow,
of Time
and of Space

Orphans
of the Titanic

Sidney F. Tyler

AZTEX Corporation, Tucson AZ 85703

ISBN 0-89404-062-6

Library of Congress Catalog Card No. 81-68385

Printed in the United States of America

AZTEX Corporation
P O Box 50046, Tucson, AZ 85703

For Lolo,
the gold at the base of The Rainbow

Contents

A Rainbow, of Time and of Space

Orphans of the Titanic

Sidney F. Tyler

Prologue

The Western Base

FORSAN ET HAEC OLIM MEMINISSE JUVABIT
The Aeneid

Photo: The Bettman Archive, Inc.

ORPHANED BY THE WRECK
When the Carpathia reached New York these two little French children were found in the care of Miss Hayes, a survivor. Their father went down with the Titanic.

Chapter One

❧ FOR AN ENTERPRISING YOUNG MAN with ambition to better his lot, prospects were not good in the dying years of the Austro-Hungarian empire. A society which was marked by great inequity in the ownership of wealth and by a rigid system of caste had little to offer to a person who sought material and social advancement. One was condemned, it must have seemed, to the circumstances which prevailed at the time of one's birth.

To the perceptive mind of Michel Navratil, these truths became apparent at an early age. He had been born in 1880 in the little town of Szered, about 40 miles east of the city now known as Bratislava, in what became Czechoslovakia after the dissolution of the Empire. His parents were of sturdy Slovak stock and saw to it that he was educated for the niche in life they expected him to fill. He was trained in the trade of a tailor and quickly became self-supporting; but he soon began to chafe under the limitations he foresaw. In the year 1902, stalwart and strong in the prime of his youth, the lure of a better

15

life in a country offering broader opportunity became irresistible, and he emigrated to France. He resumed his vocation in Nice, and began to prosper.

It was in 1906 or early 1907, while serving as an instructor in a sewing class, that Michel first met his future bride. Her name was Marcelle Carretto. She was the daughter of Italian parents, her father having come from Turin and her mother from near Genoa. Like so many Italians of the time, they had been drawn to Argentina, where her father had found work as a woodcutter; but when he later moved to Brazil, he lost his life to yellow fever. Her mother had thereupon returned to Europe and settled in Nice to await the birth of her baby, which took place in 1890. Marcelle had thus grown up with the cultural and geographic diversities which came from being French by birth and upbringing, with parents of Italian origin who had spent their early working years in South America. When Michel made her acquaintance, she had not yet reached 17 and was ten years his junior.

For a bachelor of 27 who was well established in his trade and had garnered the means to support a wife, the chance to display his skill with a needle to a willing pupil of the opposite sex must have been a source of pride and a spur to ambition. Michel saw before him a vivacious young lady in the fresh bloom of her youth and was instantly captivated. Marcelle responded to the magnet which draws pupil to teacher and which oscillates with added resonance when disparity in years adds lustre to the latter in the eyes of the former. The vision each held of the other was enriched by the contrasts in their personalities and in their cultural origins. The courtship was ardent and swift, and an early wedding was planned.

The route to the altar, however, proved more difficult than they had thought. The requirements of French law were not easy for them to satisfy, perhaps because of the bride's tender age, or reluctant parental consent, or something lacking in the proof of citizenship. Whatever the reason, the obstacles seemed formidable and complex, and the couple lost patience.

16

They knew that in Britain the laws in such matters were less strict; so Michel and Marcelle eloped to England and the rites of marriage were celebrated there.

Their first child was born in 1908. They named him Michel and gave him the sobriquet of Lolo. A second son followed in 1910, to whom they gave the name of Edmond and the knickname of Momon. The family lived in Nice where Michel prospered in his craft. Marcelle augmented the family income as a seamstress, and Marcelle's mother, Angèle, helped out with the chores and the children. In the glow of newly wedded bliss, it appeared to be a happy beginning.

But the marriage which had been launched with such romantic ardor began to suffer as the children arrived and their needs increased. Passions which once had burned at fever heat began to cool, and harmony gave way to quarrels and disagreements. Perhaps the contrast between the Slovak culture and the Mediterranean, and between the Latin character and the Slav, turned out to be less magnetic than initially hoped; perhaps the young bride did not yet possess the maturity to cope with the triple demands of motherhood, home, and work; and perhaps their disenchantment with each other came about because Marcelle was artistic, imaginative, and inclined to be impulsive, whereas Michel was decisive, determined, and at times peremptory. Matters were not helped by Michel's conviction that Angèle, through frequent disparagement, was turning his wife against him, and by his awareness that both women were virtually inseparable, in a kind of symbiotic interdependence which persisted as though the marriage had never been.

Under these circumstances, life for the Navratil family became an ordeal of mounting tension, and both parties came to the conclusion that to continue their lives together was no longer possible. Early in 1912, Michel moved to bachelor quarters and the couple filed for a separation on the grounds of incompatibility. The court awarded the children to Angèle's brother, a man named Bruno, who also lived in Nice. He, in turn, later gave them back to their mother, thereby incurring a reprimand from the court. Then Bruno, a week or so before Easter, which in that year was on April 7th, effected a reconciliation between the parents, persuading them to his view that their differences were no more than superficial. But the reconciliation lasted only three days. Time and separation had hardened positions and worsened resentments, and Michel returned to his quarters in deep dejection. Sometime during the Easter week-end, Marcelle sent her children to visit their father. When she returned to fetch them, she found to her consternation that the boys and Michel had disappeared, leaving behind them not a trace.

Chapter
Two

WEDNESDAY MORNING, APRIL 10TH, dawned bright and clear in the port of Southampton, and at earliest light its biggest pier came alive with the sights and sounds of bustling humanity. Preparations for the departure of a great vessel were well advanced, but because this was no ordinary sailing, stevedores bent to their tasks with more than their usual will; tall cranes bowed their heads with extra grace as they eased their freight into the holds below; small engines whistled with playful glee, in shrill salute to things to come; and lines of porters took pride in their pace, as they toiled with their burdens like ants on the march to their home. Over the sound and the movement hung an air of expectancy, because the ship was the TITANIC, and she was being readied for her maiden voyage.

It was an event for which the world had long been waiting. Years of meticulous planning had come to their end, and the hopes of a nation rode high upon the result. The TITANIC was not only the latest and highest expression of marine architecture; she was also the crowning achievement of Britain's maritime supremacy, of her industrial power, and of her global dominion over palm and pine. In addition, she was the quintessential image of Edwardian elegance, and a majestic witness to the pride of an empire on which the sun never set. Within the lithe perfection of her sculptured form, she offered luxury unsurpassed, in a hull whose bulkheads and interior compartmentation were such that she was believed to be unsinkable. Some would choose to sail in her for the sheer adventure of her nuptial crossing; others would do so for the glamor which inclusion in her Passenger List would convey; and still others would board her as the swiftest and safest means of reaching the New World. Whatever the reasons, the TITANIC passengers knew themselves to be participants in an event of historic importance.

The morning was well advanced when the train from London came to a stop and disgorged its throng of excited travelers. In the clamor of arrival, it is doubtful that anyone noticed the silent figure of a sturdy man with thick hair, dark eyes, and a mustache which was shaped and sharpened in the style made famous by the German Kaiser. He was standing motionless with two small boys at his side, and he seemed to be lost in thought as his eyes first swept the length of the ship then turned in wonder to the towering prow above him. For no more than a moment he stood there; and then, without a word or a gesture, he gathered his children and threaded his way through the crowd to the gangplank for Second Class. "L. Hoffman," he said laconically to the purser as he surrendered his ticket, "and two boys." The Passenger List confirmed the booking and a steward led him to his cabin.

Precisely at noon the ship's horn sounded and a bevy of tugboats began their work. Into the Solent and down past the Isle of Wight the TITANIC gathered speed. A good beginning, mused Hoffman, as he leaned on the rail and watched the shoreline recede: only one more hurdle to cross. The rhythms of vibration, and the calmness aboard which followed the confusion ashore, produced a surge of elation.

There had been, he reflected, four days of apprehension, made sharp and pungent by the fear of discovery. He had known that the police would mount a search, that he and his sons would be conspicuous targets, and that the trains and the railway stations would be closely watched. He had felt like a hunted thing on that first dash from his quarters, and later during that wakeful trip to Paris as the engine's high-pitched whistle broke the stillness of the night. Then there had been the run to the coast, through country bursting with the colors and fragrance of early spring, its enjoyment spoiled by the gnawing dread of pursuit. Not until the ferry delivered him safely to the English shore, after a crossing made miserable by mountainous seas, had he been able to feel at ease. His memories of England five years before, likewise under conditions of flight, had given him a comfortable sense of security, as if the echoes of the past had come back to reassure him in the present. Now, with Southampton embarcation safely behind him, there remained only the fear that on arrival at Cherbourg, the police would be ready and waiting.

It was nearly dark when the TITANIC dropped anchor in the outer harbor, and the sky came alive with its carpet of stars. Lights twinkled on the distant shore and Hoffman watched them with a wary eye. Presently a tender emerged from the port and set course for the liner in wait, pitching and rolling in the soft Channel swells as she approached. When she came within range of the TITANIC's lights, he could see that her deck was piled high with luggage and that masses of people were lining the rails. In helpless fascination he gazed down upon the little vessel as she settled snugly in the great ship's lee. When the gangplank was extended and the passengers began their labored climb aboard, he kept a sharp eye for uniformed police, knowing that his crucial moment had come.

For nearly two hours the tender lay alongside, and Hoffman kept watch from the darkness above. His mind was alert and his nerves were taut. As time passed and no hand was laid upon his shoulder, and no voice was heard to call his name,

21

he began to relax; and when the tender signalled her intent to depart by short blasts of her whistle and the retraction of her gangplank, his spirits rose to the level of euphoria. The raising of the anchor and the soothing pulse of the TITANIC's engines told him that the last hurdle had been crossed and that now he could look to the future with confidence.

For the first four days of the voyage, all was serene in the Hoffman family. With clear skies and moderate seas, much time was spent on deck, where the children played happily by themselves. People spoke of how attentive Hoffman was to his sons and what joy he seemed to find in being with them. Nobody presumed to ask questions; but there were some who wondered whether, in his selfless devotion, he might not be trying to make up to the boys for the recent loss of their mother.

Sunday, April 14th, seemed made to order. It was a cloudless day in which the thermometer steadily sank and the wind slackened. By dark the temperature had fallen to freezing and the breeze had dropped to nothing. The sea lay smooth as a polished mirror and the stars of a moonless night danced lightly on its surface. In conditions which seemed just short of perfection, the TITANIC raced at full speed through a lifeless ocean.

For the men on watch in the crow's nest, however, conditions were not so ideal. Binoculars furnished in Belfast had been withdrawn in Southampton, so the men made do with the naked eye. A band of haze obscured the horizon and played troublesome tricks with the sense of perspective. Their eyes grew tired as the night advanced and they were more than ready for their midnight relief.

With less than a half-hour of their watch to go, a faint gray shape loomed up ahead. As its measure was taken in sharpening focus, a peak appeared above the haze, then the massive form of its base below. "Iceberg ahead!" called the watch to the bridge, as the TITANIC closed with awesome speed. Slowly the ship altered course to port, but her response was sluggish and her momentum too great. Collision occurred at 11:40 P.M. and the TITANIC quickly came to a halt, a mortal wound in her starboard quarter.

Among the passengers, not more than a slight shudder was noted at the moment of impact, and those who were inclined to be flippant made light of the fragments of ice that covered her decks. Some continued their card games undisturbed; others merely noted that the engines had stopped and that the ship now lay dead in the water. There were muffled sounds of scurrying feet, and of cabin doors being opened and shut, but no signs of general alarm. To the inquiries of the curious, the stewards were calm and reassuring in their replies.

But Hoffman was not so easily satisfied. Not long after the collision his sense of balance warned him that the ship was down by the head, and he left his cabin to make his own investigation. As he reached the top deck his ears were assaulted by the roar of escaping steam and his eyes were dazzled by the cascading fire of exploding rockets. When crowds began to form at the boat-stations and the first lifeboats were eased over the side, it was plain that the TITANIC had not long to live. He turned abruptly and sped to his cabin, with a sickening awareness of the lives that depended upon him.

He allowed himself to be delayed, however, by a young lady in her middle teens. Her name was Madeline Mellenger and she, too, was a passenger in Second Class. He knew her because she had often played with his boys on deck, and he had been impressed by her gentle nature. As he approached his cabin, he came upon this frightened girl emerging from hers. In her haste to make her escape, she had flung a few scraps of clothing about her, and she carried her shoes in her hand. In the accounts she later gave of that night, she told of being stopped by Hoffman who warned of the bitter cold outside and insisted that she take the time to don her warmest garments. When she slipped her shoes upon her feet, he fell to his knees and tied the laces for her, unmindful of the obstruction to traffic in the corridor that his posture thus caused. She recalled how his calmness had comforted her and how grateful she was for his wise advice. For the rest of her life she cherished the memory of a thoughtful and considerate gentleman.

Hoffman had now but a single purpose. The boys must be gotten on deck at once, with maximum protection against the cold. But how to manage through the gathering crowds and up staircases that now seemed to defy the laws of gravity? He was struck by the chilling thought that he could not manage both boys at one time by himself, and that he dared not risk their separation by first taking one then the other. At all costs he must persuade someone to help him. It was at that point that a Good Samaritan entered his life.

Nothing is known of who he was, or what plans of his own he put aside. It is known only that the plea of a desperate parent prevailed and that a stranger appeared in Hoffman's cabin to help with the preparations. The two men roused the boys from their sleep and dressed them in all the warm clothing they possessed, then wrapped them in blankets torn from their beds. Hoffman led off with Lolo in his arms as the stranger followed with Momon; together they made their way to the boat-deck and surrendered their burdens at the first boat-station they reached. His good deed done, the stranger withdrew, perhaps to become a victim of his own unselfishness. There is no record of what then happened to him.

Hoffman took in the situation at a glance. Below him he saw boats already launched and pulling away from the stricken ship, like spiders struggling in an oily sea. He saw a boat before him which was making ready to descend. He realized that little time was left for him to do what he had to do.

It is a common experience that in moments of high drama, the human mind recalls, with a vividness which never pales, the smallest details of great events. Such a moment was the imminent lowering of one of the last lifeboats to leave the ship, and there were some persons in whose memories the scene about to be enacted was indelibly etched. Survivors remembered the distant sounds of the ship's orchestra playing current rag-time favorites, the canopy of bright stars that hung sparkling overhead, and the great silence which gripped so

24

eloquently the waiting throng. There were women and children settling themselves as best they could in the cramped quarters of the boat; there were men who stood wistfully at the ready, hoping against hope that space might be found for them; and there were those who, mindful of the ship's rumored unsinkability, shrank from what seemed to be the greater risks of a cockleshell turned loose upon an open ocean, preferring instead to take their chances with a vessel which they hoped might somehow survive. Suddenly they became aware of Hoffman before them, his boys at his side. The recollection of what happened remained very clear in the minds of those who saw, and lived to tell of it.

They remembered Hoffman down on his knees, making sure that each child was tightly wrapped. The younger boy was so thoroughly bundled that he could scarcely move, and lay prone and inert upon the deck. The older boy, equally well covered, stood patiently beside him. They saw Hoffman, still on his knees, gather this boy in a close embrace, rivet his gaze on the youngster's eyes, and speak to him with passionate intensity. "My child," he said, "when your mother comes for you, as she surely will, tell her that I loved her dearly and still do. Tell her that I expected her to follow us, so that we might all live happily together in the peace and freedom of the New World."

Witnesses saw Hoffman give Lolo a farewell kiss, then thrust him quickly into the hands of a sailor standing in the boat. They recalled its uneven descent toward the sea as tackle groaned and pulleys creaked, and the perilous angle at which the little craft hung. They saw him turn to his second son, fold him close in a last farewell, then drop him into the waiting arms of passengers now many feet below; and they remembered that he followed with his eyes the boat's rough landing in the water and the first wild strokes of its oars, to assure himself that all was well. They never forgot his moving salute as he slipped backward into the silent crowd, or the look of resignation which settled on his face. They sensed that he was at peace with himself and ready for whatever was to come.

He was never seen alive again. Soon after the launching of the last of her boats, the TITANIC plunged to her doom. Five days later his floating body, fully clothed and sustained by his life-jacket, was recovered by the cableship MACKAY-BENNETT and taken to that section of the graveyard in Halifax set aside for the victims of the tragedy. A simple headstone now marks his grave. On it are the words:

MICHEL NAVRATIL
DIED

APRIL $^{15,}_{16,}$ 1912

Chapter Three

❧ THE R.M.S. CARPATHIA OF THE CUNARD LINE, under the command of Capt. Arthur H. Rostron, was en route to the Mediterranean when her wireless picked up the distress calls of the TITANIC. Without a moment's hesitation, the Captain ordered that course be altered and that his ship proceed at maximum speed to the scene of the disaster, regardless of icebergs known to be in the vicinity. The CARPATHIA closed the 58 miles that separated the two vessels in a little over four hours. She picked up the first boatload of survivors at 4:10 A.M. of Monday, April 15th, and continued rescue operations until 8:30 A.M. when the last boat was recovered. Among the last was that which held Lolo and Momon. The boys had survived the intense cold of their seven hours adrift in part because of the care with which their father had prepared them, and in part because of the nourishment given them by a fellow survivor. Mr. Hugh Woolner had stuffed his pockets with crackers before leaving the TITANIC and claimed with pride that he had dispensed them throughout the night to the children at his feet. Since there were some persons who later died of exposure after their ordeal in the boats, his assertion that his bounty had saved their lives cannot be totally rejected.

Another survivor in the lifeboat with the boys was a young lady named Margaret Hays. She had been educated in France and spoke French fluently. Because her cabin had been in First Class on the TITANIC, it is doubtful that she had ever seen the Hoffman boys before she found herself in the same boat with them; but she must have observed the dramatic manner in which their father propelled them to safety. From her fellow passengers she learned their family name. Their plight, and her understanding of what Lolo occasionally said, aroused her special sympathy and led her to assume the role of foster mother. The children were never to forget the love and care which, from the moment of rescue, she lavished upon them.

It was fortunate that the CARPATHIA had sailed with only half her cabins filled. As Miss Hays climbed the ladder and entered the vitals of the ship, she requested and was given a room large enough for the children and herself. The boys soon followed aboard, being lifted from lifeboat to liner in a canvas bucket normally used to jettison ashes. Somehow, in the feverish activity of reception, while identification was being made and while food, blankets, and clothing were being issued, the children got separated, with one being left in Cabin Class and the other being taken to Steerage. The howls of distress that burst from the lungs of both boys bore witness to their vitality and led, after a brief delay, to their being reunited, at which time their fears of being lost to each other were allayed. Thereafter, they were never apart, and never out of sight of their surrogate parent.

As life on the CARPATHIA settled into its new routines, the matter of identity became of paramount concern. Where did these Hoffman children come from, and who were their next of kin? How might their relatives be found, and what had become of their mother? Momon was still too young to speak coherently; and while Lolo could converse at the level which was normal of a child not yet four, he was inclined to be silent and introspective, and there was little Miss Hays could glean from him concerning his past. To be sure, there were occasional references to Papa and Maman; but Lolo revealed no comprehension of his father's fate, and nothing he said threw light on the status of his mother. Nevertheless, Miss Hays began to perceive certain things which were later to prove helpful.

She noticed, for example, their heavy black hair, their dark eyes, and their sallow complexion, which together suggested generations of exposure to the sun. Her ear began to detect certain shades of pronunciation not heard in Paris but reminiscent of the South. The combination of complexion and speech made her suspect that they were of Mediterranean stock; and when she happened to ask Lolo if he had ever heard of Nice, the boy confirmed her suspicions by exclaiming, "Oh, that is where Maman lives!"

There were things about their deportment that intrigued her. She was struck by their good manners and their commitment to established routines. She noticed that, in accordance with the prevailing custom in Europe of the time, the children did not speak at table unless spoken to. She observed their insistence upon having their daily baths at the same hour each day, and the faithful recitation of their prayers at bed-time. She was amused, too, to note how once in the dining-saloon Lolo reacted with vigor to the discovery that napkins had not been provided and his demand that they be produced. From little things like these, Miss Hays concluded that the children must have come from the kind of family in which discipline was firm and consistent, and where the essentials of good manners were taught and insisted upon at an early age.

Chapter
Four

❧ THANKS TO THE AMPLE FACILITIES of the transatlantic
cables and to Marconi's recent invention of wireless telegraphy, the news of the greatest maritime disaster in history
was quickly spread across the world. Newspapers in Europe
and America reported the event in their biggest headlines and
boldest type, and spared no effort to record every detail. Of
transcendent importance was the identity of those saved and,
by inference, those lost. The TITANIC was known to have had
2,208 souls on board; the CARPATHIA's wireless required
two days to transmit the names and addresses of the rescued;
and when, on the morning of Wednesday the 17th, her listing
ended at a total of 705 recovered, it became apparent that 1,503
persons were not accounted for and must be presumed lost.
An anguished public awaited each news release with bated
breath, fed avidly on the details, mourned for the victims,
and rejoiced at the safety of those alive. Included among the
latter, toward the end of the roster and without supporting
detail, were the names of two Hoffman boys, whose plight

aroused immediate and world-wide concern.

To Marcelle Navratil, at home in Nice and absorbed in the search for her missing sons, the news that monopolized the front pages of the newspapers was of dramatic but impersonal interest. Her thoughts were engrossed to the limit with her quest for clues and her efforts to assist the police; but like everyone else, she scanned the daily lists of those reported saved. On or about Thursday the 18th her eyes fell upon the mention of two boys bearing the name of Hoffman, and she began to wonder.

In New York, a frenzy of preparation to meet the returning vessel was under way. Committees had been formed and large sums of money had been raised to provide food and shelter, emergency clothing, medical services, and whatever else might be needed for the relief of destitute survivors. Barricades to control crowds had been put in place, reserves of police had been mobilized to keep order and restrain the impetuous, and fleets of cabs had been requested to stand by. With a compassionate regard for the plight of the rescued, the Immigration Service had agreed to relax its normal procedures for the admission of aliens and to substitute a bare minimum of formalities. All was in readiness when, at 9:35 P.M. of Thursday the 18th, the CARPATHIA inched her way into dock. When Miss Hays disembarked with her two French children in tow, she waved aside all offers of assistance and was permitted to pass unhindered through the crowds. A taxi took her to her apartment at 304 West 83rd Street.

On Friday the 19th, Miss Hays must have yielded to the demands of the press because the New York Times of Saturday the 20th reports an interview with her, presumably in her apartment. Photographers were present, and a picture by Underwood & Underwood was later published which showed the two little boys dressed in their nightclothes and seated together in the corner of the sofa, Momon a bit perplexed and Lolo smiling broadly. Miss Hays gave the facts of her association with the children and what little else she knew about them. She spoke of their ready acceptance of their new life, and joked that the first thing they asked for when they woke up that morning was their bath. In the middle of this ritual, said she, Momon inquired of his brother: "Where's Papa?" From Lolo came the laconic answer: "He's gone." Miss Hays saw this as the first sign that the loss of their father had been acknowledged, and that Lolo had now brought himself to accept the tragedy.

Proof of the widespread interest in what the press had come to call "The Orphans of the Deep" made itself felt from the moment of arrival. Offers to adopt them descended upon Miss Hays in great numbers, some by telephone, many by mail, and even a few by personal solicitation. She referred all requests to The Children's Aid Society and made it known that none would be considered until all possibilities of discovering their next of kin had been exhausted. The search for them would be her primary concern, she said, and she was confident they could be found. To look after the children in the meantime, and to help her fend off both serious applicants and those who intruded from sheer curiosity, Miss Hays obtained from the Society the services of an English trained nurse by the name of Miss Utley, who proceeded to deal admirably with the problems of care and custody.

There was another concern for Miss Hays, which was probably resolved before the visit of the press on the 19th: the children were destitute and had to be clothed. She took them to Franklin, Simon & Co. at 414 Fifth Avenue. There an alert clerk suspected their identity and informed the management, whereupon an official appeared and insisted that his company be permitted, as its contribution to the relief of TITANIC survivors, to equip each child with a complete wardrobe, free of charge. The offer was gratefully accepted; it may have been part of the donor's bounty which the boys were seen wearing when they were later photographed.

Chapter Five

❧ THE LOGICAL MAN in New York for Miss Hays to approach in launching her search was the French Consul-General, M. Étienne Lanel. It was to him that friends and relatives of French TITANIC passengers appealed, on both sides of the Atlantic, and his office fast became a clearing-house for all the facts as they developed. It is possible that Miss Hays may have reached him as early as Friday the 19th, and it is certain that the information she gave him provoked his interest and challenged his imagination. He would like to come to her apartment and see the boys for himself, he said; and he promised to do so as soon as the pressures upon him relaxed and he could take time to escape from his office. Meanwhile, he said, there were questions which should be asked immediately of the White Star Line and he would urge its New York office to give them their best attention. Had they, for example, any record of an address for Hoffman? Or, failing that, what was the number of his ticket and where and by whom was it issued? Could the agent furnish a description of the man to whom he sold it? These questions were promptly cabled to London, where officials of the Line, desperate to do everything in their power to help, promised their fullest cooperation. No doubt the substance of these inquiries did not escape the notice of the press.

It was probably on the afternoon of Saturday the 20th that Lanel arrived at Miss Hays' apartment. He had been wondering what questions he could ask of a boy three months short of being four that might produce some useful clues. It occurred to him that Easter that year had been on April 7th, and that if the family had celebrated the occasion in the customary manner, something of value might be learned. After the usual preliminaries aimed at putting the boys at their ease, he turned to Lolo and the following conversation took place:

Lanel: "Easter was only a little while ago. Do you remember anything about it?"

Lolo: "Yes, I do."

Lanel: "What do you remember in particular?"

Lolo: "The present I received."

Lanel: "What kind of a present was it?"

Lolo: "A chicken."

Lanel: "A chicken! What kind of a chicken?"

Lolo: "It was a chicken with real feathers."

Lanel: "And what did this chicken do?"

Lolo: "It laid eggs."

Lanel: "It did? What kind of eggs?"

Lolo, with a broad grin: "Chocolate eggs."

To Lanel, this was interesting, but hardly productive. He continued with other questions and learned that Lolo's mother was called Marcelle, that he often stayed at the home of his grandmother in Nice, and that she was not well. When Lanel returned to his office, he was satisfied that he had extracted all the information he could, and he regretted that it was not of greater substance. In deference to the world's appetite for even the smallest details concerning the TITANIC and its passengers, he released the conversation in its entirety to the press and thought no more about it. In due course it was reported verbatim in the newspapers of the world.

Meanwhile, the London office of the White Star Line had not been idle. The Company did have a record of Hoffman's ticket number, which they traced to the Monte Carlo office of Thos. Cook & Sons, and the information was promptly made public. The British consul at Nice was requested to obtain all possible information concerning the buyer, but his inquiry produced nothing. Thos. Cook could furnish no address for Hoffman and the Consul concluded that there was nothing more that he could do.

Unknown to the Consul, however, was the suspicion which Marcelle had begun to feel on Thursday the 18th when she first saw the names of two Hoffman boys among the rescued. It was an intuitive reaction which fed upon itself and gained in urgency each passing hour. When, therefore, she read the details of Lanel's April 20th interview in her newspaper of the 22nd, suspicion hardened into conviction. Could there be any other mother in all France who had given her sons an Easter present of this nature only to have them disappear so shortly afterward, she asked herself? And if, a fortnight later, they were included in the roster of TITANIC survivors as orphans of origin unknown, must not their father have been bound for America and have paid the price with his life? Then all at once the aptness of the Hoffman name struck sharply home: she had a friend and neighbor called Louis Hoffman; and Michel, to foil the police by the false registration of his ticket, had purloined the name. To Marcelle, the evidence was overwhelming and it remained only for her to establish that the buyer of the ticket had been her husband.

Accordingly, she appealed to the British consul. She gave him a picture of Michel and asked him to show it to the individual in Thos. Cook who had sold the ticket. Since not many tickets on the TITANIC had been sold by the Monte Carlo office, and since the face of a stalwart man with waxed and sharpened mustache was not easily forgotten, recognition was immediate and her suspicion of Michel's alias was confirmed.

With all doubt now removed, Marcelle cabled her claim to Lanel and repeated to the London office of the White Star Line, together with a request for the earliest possible passage to New York. The Times of Wednesday the 24th reported the claim and stated that the Line accepted it. The next day she was offered free passage in Second Class together with similar free passage for herself and her children on the return voyage. The vessel chosen was the OCEANIC, which was due to sail from Cherbourg on May 8th and to leave New York on the homeward run on May 18th. Although she was disappointed that an earlier sailing from France could not be arranged, Marcelle gratefully accepted the offer, with a tidal wave of relief at the knowledge that in little more than a fortnight she and her sons would be reunited.

Marcelle had still to establish her claim with Miss Hays as the children's rightful parent. She knew that Miss Hays had received and rejected many offers of adoption and she felt certain that extreme vigilance would be used in guarding against impostors. In consequence, Marcelle sought the Paris representative of a New York paper and through him sent to Miss Hays a complete description of the children, mentioning in particular their scars and physical peculiarities. This must have been done just before April 26th because the Saturday Globe of Utica reported in its issue of the 27th that Miss Hays had accepted Marcelle's credentials and had gone on to say that, "The little chaps have all the charm of babyhood and are decidedly handsome as well. They are the smartest and loveliest little fellows in the world."

Miss Hays, too, rejoiced that identification had been made, and that the agony of Marcelle's long ordeal was now about to end. It did so with the early morning arrival of the OCEANIC in New York on Thursday, May 16th.

Chapter Six

❧ AMONG THE MANY WHO FOLLOWED the fortunes of the TITANIC survivors was a young French lady named Rose Bruno. She was the daughter of that same Bruno, Marcelle's uncle, to whom the court had awarded the Navratil children in the decree of separation, and she was therefore Marcelle's first cousin. She had come to America in search of a living and had found employment as a governess. In April, 1912, she was working in the suburbs of Philadelphia in a small community called Elkins Park. Her employer was my mother, and her duty was to look after my sister and me. The former was not yet two at the time and I lacked a few months of being five. Mlle Bruno, as we formally addressed her, was a warm and motherly person, and I think of her with great affection.

The moment of arrival of Lolo and Momon at our family home I do not remember, but I clearly recall their presence there and the happy times we spent together. The house in which we lived was built in the Georgian style of red brick with white trim; and its dimensions suggested that when my parents approved the plans, at the time of their marriage in 1905, they had made provision for a larger family than was later to eventuate. My parents must also have believed in the virtues of self-sufficiency, because the modest acreage they possessed contained a large kitchen garden, a small dairy with enough cows to satisfy our needs, pear trees and apple trees the forbidden fruit of which I shall never forget, and all the paraphernalia required for the raising of ducks and chickens, including an incubator for fertile eggs whose miraculous output was a constant fascination. Over this little world of bursting life presided a humorless Scot by the name of Fred Sellers, who at certain times seemed unexplainably irascible and at other times, when the mood was upon him, was graciously pleased to suffer little boys to "help" him with his chores. Lolo and I, with Momon at our heels, made the most of the many pleasures which this bucolic life provided.

I do not know the actual date on which the Navratil boys first came to us, but I suspect that it must have been very early in the month of May. Nor do I know the precise chain of events which led to their arrival. Nothing in the newspapers of the time throws light on this; and if there was ever any communication between Marcelle and Rose on the subject, either by cable or by letter, none of it survives. I therefore surmise that Rose, having followed the story of her young cousins as it developed in the press, appealed to my mother to give them asylum; that upon receipt of permission she went to New York to submit her credentials to The Children's Aid Society and to Miss Hays; and that having convinced them of her authenticity, she brought them back to Elkins Park on one of the hourly trains that then connected New York and Philadelphia. How much advance notice was required to make appointments, or whether she took her chances and left without benefit of appointments, cannot now be determined. All that we can be sure of is that her affectionate nature and her strong sense of family ties impelled her to take charge of the children with utmost speed.

The time arrives when all idylls must come to an end, and in our case that time came on Wednesday, May 15th, when Rose took the boys back to New York to meet their mother. The reunion took place on Thursday the 16th and was extensively covered in the Times of the following day. From it I quote:

Four-year-old Michel and two-year-old Edmond Navratil, the two waifs who were saved from the sinking TITANIC and brought to this city under the temporary guardianship of Miss Margaret Hays of 304 West Eighty-Third Street, another survivor, are waifs no longer. They have a mother now, just like other children of less romantic and adventurous infancy.

She came on the White Star liner OCEANIC to claim them yesterday; and mother and waifs alike, the former an adult, and the latter in baby-prattle French, insisted over and over again, all day long, that there would never be another parting. That was about all they did say from early morning until night, and they were talking and babbling industriously to each other in sprightly baby-code practically all the time.

Mme Marcelle Navratil, the mother, is herself only twenty-one years old, and is as pretty as the two children whose pictures have since been admired by newspaper readers in every country of the world. She is rather slender, lithe, and graceful, with a wealth of lustrous black hair, big brown eyes, and a complexion of peach-bloom. She wore deep mourning yesterday, and dark shadows under her eyes told of the many days and nights of yearning she had spent for her children since first she learned of their fate and came to recover them in a strange land. She had mingled little with the other passengers on the OCEANIC, except with one American woman who spoke French; and to her the mother had told her story, centering always around the children. Her chief anxiety seemed to be: Would they recognize her?

The father of Miss Margaret Hays, Mr. Frank K. Hays,

Miss Hays herself, and Miss Utley, the trained nurse who had taken care of the little ones, met Mme Navratil at the White Star pier. There, too, were Supt. Walsh of The Children's Aid Society, and Mlle Rose Bruno, a cousin of Mme Navratil, who had taken the children to Elkins Park, Penn., where she is employed as a governess, and who brought them back yesterday to the rooms of the Society to await their mother. There was a fond embrace between the two kinswomen, and then Miss Hays was introduced to Mme Navratil. Weeping, the young mother embraced her. The two women spoke softly together in French. The mother asked about Michel, the solemn elder of the two, and then about Edmond, who was the more demonstrative one.

Mme Navratil was detained only a short time by Customs formalities about her baggage. She had only two pieces, a small suitcase and a little valise. Mr. Hays carried these, and the party then hurried in two taxicabs to the Society's headquarters. In the street they encountered a small army of photographers and reporters; and the windows of the building opposite were lined with interested groups of shopworkers who had got wind of what was happening across the way and who were craning their necks and gesticulating wildly toward a window on the fifth floor, where the children were believed to be.

Mr. Hays and Supt. Walsh helped the young mother from the taxicab and hurried her past the photographers into the building. Then the party hastened upstairs to the nurses' parlor on the fifth floor, where the children were. At the door, the rest of the party fell back, leaving Mme Navratil to enter alone. Timorously she stopped a moment, with hand on the doorknob. Then, quickly, she opened the door and entered.

Michel was sitting in the corner on the window-seat, with a big-pictured alphabet book in his lap. Edmond was scrambling over the floor, awkwardly trying to piece together a puzzle picture, and crowing contentedly in a language no one but he could understand.

It didn't take a second. Off from his window-seat slid

42

Monsieur Michel, and instantly Monsieur Edmond, on all fours, strove his utmost to scramble to his feet. Both looked frightened. Then, a growing wonder spread over the serious face of the bigger boy, while the smaller one, now happily righted on his sturdy legs, stared in wide amazement at the figure in the doorway. He let out one long-drawn and lusty wail and ran blubbering into the outstretched arms of his mother.

The mother was trembling with sobs and her eyes were dim with tears as she ran forward and seized both youngsters. Michel, too, had darted toward her, sobbing for all he was worth. But when he saw that his mother, too, was weeping he turned his face and put the back of one hand before his eyes to conceal his tears, while she hugged and kissed him. Little Edmond, his face buried in his mother's breast, was howling, "Oh, Maman! Oh, Maman!" as if his heart would break, while the elder of the two little men, clinging to the maternal neck, chorused the same greeting in softer and more dignified but not less honest sobs. Those who had stood at the door closed it gently and remained unobtrusively outside.

Mme Navratil and her two boys were left alone in the room for nearly an hour. After a while their friends heard laughter break through the tears and then one continuous and ever-increasing babble of baby French. It was stated on the best French authority, afterward, that there had not been a single serious or sensible word said by mother or children in all that time.

Later, when Mme Navratil and her babies were interviewed by a score of men and women introduced as "la presse," she declared that she had not asked the children a single thing about their experiences on shipboard or thereafter, nor about their father, who had parted with them on the TITANIC and gone to his death with the ship.

"I do not want them to think about that," she said. "They must only be happy from now on — only happy; no more distress."

As a matter of fact, when the reporters finally did get into the room, it was Michel who received them. He was standing alone near the window, his back to the windowsill and a big picture-book in one hand. The index finger of the other hand was in his mouth as he gazed with questioning eyes at the newcomers. He measured them solemnly from top to toe, one after another, and waited for them to speak.

"Bon jour, mon petit," one of the women reporters said.

"Bon jour," replied Michel briefly, holding forth one hand to her. And then he measured her, too.

Mme Navratil turned now, with Edmond clinging to her skirts and crowing merrily. A moment later he discovered a telephone book on the floor and got busy turning its leaves, still laughing and gurgling with contentment. He was the prattler of the two; Michel was the quiet, serious, little old man. Mme Navratil was asked whether the children had changed since she last saw them. She thought they had grown a bit thinner and that there was just a trifle less red under the olive satin of their cheeks.

Continually she was running her fingers through the curly hair of the babies as she spoke. A mist of tears arose in her eyes when she mentioned Miss Hays' name. Her gratitude to the rescuer of her children, she said, could not be put into words; she could never, never forget it.

Michel was tracing with his finger the outline of a boat on the page devoted to the letter B in his picture alphabet book. Mme Navratil was asked whether she had any plans as to what she would make of the boy; whether Michel, who even now wore a tan sailor suit, and who, she was told, had throughout his stay at the Hays home played with a toy steamship, would become a seaman.

"No," she replied. "He loves boats — see, even now he has picked out the picture of the boat first of all. But I want him to have nothing further to do with ships. He says he likes boats, but not airships. He is afraid of falling. He once saw an airman fall from an airplane at Nice."

"Voici une petite fille," interrupted Michel, pointing to a brightly colored picture of a little girl in the alphabet book and showing thereby his second preference, if it were to be a question of his principal interests. And Edmond, chiming in, babbled in a tongue that only his mother could understand: "Voici un petit garçon," pointing to a boy in the book.

"I'm afraid they will both be frightened when they see the big ship on which I am to take them back on Saturday," said Mme Navratil. "As for me, of course, I am not frightened, not at all."

She was asked if she would heed any of the many offers of adoption that have been made since the children reached here.

"Not on your life!" she snorted. "I couldn't give them up." She dismissed the foolish question by seizing her boys and crushing them in her embrace.

It must have been a vast relief to Marcelle when the press withdrew and she could have the children to herself.

Chapter
Seven

❧ IN ITS ISSUE OF SATURDAY THE 18TH, the Times reported
that Marcelle was so completely worn out by the emotions
of the reunion that it had been necessary to put her under the
care of the Children's Aid Society physician. At her request,
she was kept there in seclusion, to the keen disappointment of
more than one hundred persons who had called at the Society's
headquarters in the hope of seeing the mother and her children prior to their return to France. Here she received scores
of letters, all of them friendly and sympathetic, offering to
adopt her children and give them the most tender care in the
event the mother were unable to provide for them. "All use-
less," Marcelle kept saying of them, "There is nothing that
can separate us now. We are going back home to Nice forever."

There was one rather pompous proposition which was not
without humor. It was written in French, as follows: "My
sympathy for you and the children is very sincere. I am not
shiftless. My ancestors disembarked in America in 1658.
Since then we have remained French by blood and heart. Mine

always beats at the name of France. It could thus be a very great pleasure if you would allow me to see you. Will you? Don't telephone, because our telephone boy is rather stupid."

Another letter could have had more than one interpretation. "I am with you in my thoughts," it said. "I have followed step by step your painful Calvary. You have traversed the ocean and must need other things than affectionate protestations. If you desire to remain in New York, I can offer you a position which will forthwith yield you a good income and an excessively bright situation. I feel that this sentiment of profound sympathy, having been given by the exigencies of love, should be interpreted otherwise than by words. I ask you to kiss the children for me."

Rose Bruno herself had offered to adopt the children. Both boys were very fond of her, and Momon especially so. It was with no little pride that she recounted that when Marcelle had said to Lolo that she was going back to Nice, Lolo declared: "I want to go with Maman"; but that Momon had instantly countered in his baby French: "Je veux rester avec Cousine Rose." For a brief, impulsive moment, the wishes of the family were not entirely unanimous.

Among those who called in person at the Society's office was a certain Rudolph Navratil, who lived in New York and wanted to see Marcelle for the purpose of ascertaining whether her husband was related to him. With great indignation Marcelle sent word that she knew nothing about her husband's family connections and that she did not care to discuss the matter with him.

In her short two days in New York, Marcelle's euphoria was broken only once. In the words of Supt. Walsh: "The sole unpleasant feature of the entire case was the insistent demand by a representative of a moving picture concern for permission to subject the mother and children to the cinematograph." The Society declined to permit the unfortunate Navratil children to be thus exploited, and Mme Navratil expressed horror at the intrusion. She refused absolutely to see the agent of this concern, saying that "she did not desire her children to be made the subject of any sensation."

On the afternoon of Friday the 17th, Marcelle felt so much better that Supt. Walsh decided to treat the family to some of the sights of New York. With a French-speaking representative of the Society in charge, they were put in a touring car and driven up Fifth Avenue, through Central Park, and along Riverside Drive. On their way home, they stopped at the apartment of Miss Hays to say good-bye. Lolo was visibly moved, stroking her face with his hands and snuggling close against her, without saying a word. "You will never forget this beautiful young lady, will you?" said his mother. "No indeed," came the reply. "Elle est ma bien aimée." She is my best-beloved.

No one would miss the Navratil lads more than the officials and nurses of the Children's Aid Society, where they had made their home for three nights. Other children kept there, it was said, cry and fret at times, but these two never did. Nor did they ever display ill manners or bad temper. Momon was always babbling and singing to himself, and kept the nurses at their wits end trying to find enough books and pictures for his amusement. Lolo, however, was more self-sufficient and was an even greater favorite, suggesting a certain element of mystery. He seemed to be so very young, and yet so solemn, dignified, and pensive. One of the attendants said of him. "He is more like a born aristocrat than the son of a working man brought up in simple surroundings."

Late on the morning of Saturday the 18th, there was a final session with the press. The OCEANIC was due to sail at noon, and a dozen reporters were on hand when the family arrived at the pier. Marcelle led the procession on board, dressed in deep mourning and heavily veiled. She looked pale and walked slowly, with weariness. Momon was carried by a man from the Society and Lolo by one of the stewards. Rose brought up the rear, laden with books and toys given by the nurses and the general public and with bouquets of flowers

49

sent to the young mother. She was red of face and short of breath, and struggled to control her emotions. The party settled down in the Second Class saloon, where arrangements had been made for the interview. Marcelle explained that she was very tired from the excitement of the last few days and that she wanted nothing so much as a good rest. "But everyone has been so kind to me and my children," she said, "that I cannot sufficiently express my gratitude to all: to The Children's Aid Society which took care of my boys, to the press which helped so much to bring us together, to Cousin Rose who was so good to them, and above all to Miss Hays who saved them. It causes me great pain to part with all these people, great pain indeed. I cannot thank them enough."

The signal bell for "All Ashore!" was rung, and the horn of the OCEANIC sounded its double-bass warning. Hawsers were cast loose from their stanchions and the ship began to vibrate with the first turns of her propellors. Effortlessly the vessel slid out into the harbor and set course in an easterly direction, toward the beckoning arch of The Rainbow.

Epilogue
The Eastern Base

Chapter One

❦ IT WAS IN THE FALL OF 1978 that I began to reach back over the years into the hidden closets of my memory. Michel and Edmond had vanished from my life without leaving behind any record of who they were or where they had gone, but I retained a glow from their visit which the passage of time had not erased. I felt a compulsion to find them; and if my search were to prove to be too late, I wanted at least to learn the story of their lives and what kind of people they had become.

We must surely have talked about them that spring and summer of 1912 in nostalgic moments at home, but always as the Momon and Lolo we remembered. I recall no mention of the Hoffman or Navratil names, and if Marcelle ever wrote to my parents, I was never told of it. When Rose Bruno left our employ, she took with her the only source we might have had of Navratil names and addresses. I grew up, therefore, with a precious recollection, but no means whatsoever of bringing it back to life.

In 1955, Mr. Walter Lord published his absorbing story

of the TITANIC in a book called, "A Night to Remember." I read it that year with fascination, and with astonishment, because I found in the text a few words about the Hoffman boys and the Navratil family to which they belonged. When, in 1978, I asked Mr. Lord if he had any further information concerning them, he replied in the negative and referred me to a Mr. Edward S. Kamuda, the Secretary of The Titanic Historical Society. Thus began the chain of events which led to this story.

Mr. Kamuda informed me that both boys were believed to have been alive as recently as 1970, and that one was thought to have been a college professor and the other a physician. He expressed great interest in my project and furnished me with the names and addresses of certain survivors, mostly French, who were still alive and might have information of use to me. To each of them I wrote, but their replies gave me no clues. I then asked a friend who was visiting in Paris to inspect the telephone book but he reported that no Navratils were listed there. Next I wrote to our consul in Nice, who answered that there was nobody by that name in his area. A letter to our embassy in Paris produced no reply. When I appealed to the French embassy in Washington, I was politely told that they were forbidden to engage in a search for missing French persons unless such persons were blood relatives of Americans. Every avenue I explored seemed to lead to a dead end, and I did not know what to do.

Then one day I received a postcard from Mr. Kamuda in which he gave me the name and address of a Professor José Sourillan, who was reputed to have had an interview with a French lady who survived. "You might write to him about the French boys and see if he can help in some way," wrote Mr. Kamuda. "Can't hurt to try." Accordingly, I did, as follows:

Professeur José Sourillan   March 17, 1979
74 Rue des Bourguignons
92600 Asnières, France

Mon cher Professeur:

M Edouard Kamuda, du TITANIC HISTORICAL SOCI-
ETY, m'a dit que vous connaissez une dame Française qui est
une survivante du Titanic, et je vous écrit cette lettre pour vous
demander si vous voudrez bien m'envoyer son nom et son
addresse. Je vous demande cette faveur parceque je cherche
des renseignements de la famille Navratil, et c'est possible que
la dame de votre connaissance pourrez m'obliger. M Kamuda
m'a dit qu'il croyez qu'un frère étai un médecin et l'autre un
professeur. Peut-être vous avez des renseignements vous même,
et pourrez m'aider.

La raison que je cherche ces messieurs, ou leurs familles,
est qu'ils sont venu chez nous, à Philadelphie, après le Titanic
a coulé, dans le mois d'avril, 1912. Ils s'appelait Momon et
Lolo, et je crois que leurs noms étai des sobriquets pour Louis
et Michel. Leur père étai Michel Navratil; il a noyez sur le
paquebot. A ce temps, ces enfants avait a peu près deux ans
et quatre ans. Moi, j'avait cinq ans. Je me souviens très bien
de leur visite et de les plaisirs que nous avions ensemble. Je
désire re-faire leur connaissance si je peu découvrir où ils sont.
Si vous aurez la bonté de me rendre assistance, je serai très
heureux, et très reconnaissant.

Sans doute cette lettre contiens beaucoup d'erreurs d'épel-
lation et de grammaire. Et sans doute, aussi, je ne m'exprime
pas avec la facilité que l'importance du sujet demande. Pour
toutes mes imperfections, je vous demande pardon. Tandis
que je peu parler et lire en Français assez bien, j'ai oublié
presque tout ce que je savait de l'écriture, après le cours de
soixante ans.

Veuillez agréer, cher Monsieur, a l'expression de mes
meilleurs sentiments.*

*Dear Professor:

Mr. Edward Kamuda, of The Titanic Historical Society, has told me that you are acquainted with a French lady who is a survivor of the TITANIC, and I am writing you this letter to ask if you will kindly send me her name and address. I ask this favor of you because I am looking for news of the Navratil family, and it is possible that the lady you know might be able to help me. Mr. Kamuda has told me that he thinks that one brother is a physician and the other a professor. Perhaps you have knowledge of your own, and could help me.

The reason I seek these gentlemen, or their families, is that they came to us in Philadelphia, after the TITANIC sank, in the month of April, 1912. They were called Momon and Lolo, and I think that these were nicknames for Louis and Michel. Their father was Michel Navratil; he was drowned with the ship. At the time, these children were about 2 and 4. I myself was 5. I remember their visit well and the fun that we had together. I would like to re-make their acquaintance if I can find out where they are. If you will have the kindness to help me, I shall be very happy, and very grateful.

No doubt this letter contains many errors of spelling and grammar. And no doubt, too, I do not express myself with the ease which the importance of the subject demands. For all my imperfections, I offer my apologies. Whereas I can speak and read French reasonably well, I have forgotten nearly everything I once knew about the writing of it, after the lapse of sixty years.

Please accept, dear Sir, this expression of my best regards.

This letter produced an immediate reply from M Sourillan, as follows:

"Many thanks to you for your letter!

"I am a radio producer very interested in sound archives and I do have in my files the voice of a survivor of the Titanic. This person was recorded in 1953 but I never met her. I do not know any French family which had anything to do with the disaster.

"Yet, your letter was so interesting that I got interested in finding the Navratil family: I could find the address of Professor Michel Navratil through the syndicate of French doctors in Paris: This is the address:

> Michel Navratil
> 9 Rue Pasteur — Montpellier 34000
> France, tel 154 07 99

I am afraid Louis** is dead now.

"I hope these information will be of help to you, I remain, Sir

Yours respectfully   Good luck

"NB I just have had a telephone conversation with Michel. He is very enthousiast of getting in touch with you!"

**Edmond

Michel was indeed enthusiastic. It struck me like a thunderbolt when I received a letter from him dated March 29th, stating that Sourillan had sent him mine of the 17th. He apologizes for writing me in French and explains that he knows Italian and some German, but no English. He acknowledges that he is, or was, the Lolo of long ago, and laments the death of his brother Momon in 1953. He tells me that he is deeply touched to know that I still think of him and wish to renew our ancient friendship, and that as a result of my letter, he, too, has the same desire. He had written Miss Hays just after the war seeking information concerning her and us, and had presumed that the letter got lost because it produced no reply. Since Miss Hays was his only American contact, he did not know how to find us.

Michel continued with a thumbnail sketch of his life and the lives of his family. He married a student of Philosophy in 1933 and they lived happily together until her death in 1970. His mother, Marcelle, died in 1974, and he acknowledges that his debt to both women is very great. As to his own career, he states that from the beginning of his last year in high school, in 1926, he devoted himself to the study of philosophy, which he later taught in the Ile de France and in the Alps. He published his doctoral thesis in 1952 and thereupon moved to the University of Montpellier where he served as Professor of Psychology on the Faculty of Letters until his retirement in 1969. He has one son and two daughters, all of whom are married and have children. His son is Henri and his daughter-in-law is Francoise. The former is a urologist and the latter a gynecologist; both teach on the Faculty of Medicine at Montpellier and maintain an active practice on the side. His elder daughter, Michèle, is a practicing psychoanalyst and is married to an engineer. His younger daughter, Élisabeth, is a translator of German and a music critic besides. Her husband teaches History of Art on the Faculty of Letters at the University of Clermont-Ferrand. With so many advanced degrees to their credit, it was apparent that Michel's was a very scholarly family.

Another letter spoke briefly of Momon. All Michel told me was that he had married and lived in Lourdes, and that he had first been an interior decorator and then an architect and builder. In character he was, "courageous, active, intelligent, and affectionate." Later I learned that Edmond held the rank of sergeant in the French army and that at the outbreak of war he served somewhere in the north of France. Because of his marital status, he was offered a chance to apply for transfer to less hazardous duties in the rear, but he declined to do so, preferring to accept the risks of combat. He was captured when France fell and was sent to a prisoner-of-war camp in Germany, from which he escaped and made his way back to France. He died at the early age of 43. There was a finality to this brief account which seemed to discourage questions, and I did not pursue the matter further.

The letters between us flew thick and fast that spring, and as they did so, the somewhat guarded formality of the initial exchanges gave way to an easier tone. For my part, I began to relate the facts of the Navratil story as I then knew them, with due regard for such lingering sensitivities as reference to past misfortunes might yet provoke. When Michel acknowledged the depth and sincerity of our mutual interest by inviting my wife and me to visit him in Montpellier, as house-guests of Henri and Françoise, he wrote:

"In a certain sense, your accounts are entirely new to me, because I have few recollections before the age of 4, with the result that I have not retained a precise recollection of you. I recall two moments of my visit with your family, but not the faces of those of you who welcomed me with such affection. I remember in a very painful manner the TITANIC and in particular the night of the sinking, and my rescue aboard the CARPATHIA. But all the rest is much more hazy. Thus, the so affectionate letters I have received from you remind me of that magnificent inscription that I read on the facade of a building of the Renaissance at Lozère: 'Multa renascentur qui jam cecidere.' Many things which have been destroyed will come alive again later. It is really a renaissance for me to have these tidings from you, which will continue when we find each other in September."

Chapter
Two

❧ TO HAVE FOUND MY MAN after what had appeared to be a hopeless quest, and then through our correspondence to have achieved with him a rapport so cordial that it promised to open new doors into the closets of his very private past, made me think that some force beyond my understanding must have moved me, and that the stars in their courses had steered me to this end. As I bounded up the stairs in search of Michel's apartment at 9, Rue Pasteur and thus approached the climax to a commitment which had fast been gathering momentum, there seemed to be wings beneath my feet, and I felt myself swept up in a surge of exaltation. What thoughts, I wondered, were spinning at this moment through the mind of him who was awaiting me? Was he, too, stirred to his depths by emotions and memories of long ago? Would I be as comfortable in his company as I had been in the shelter of the written word? I spurned that still, small voice of warning which told me that anticipation can outrun reality, as awakening obliterates the dream. I rapped on the door, and as I heard the approaching steps within, I had the feeling that I stood, for a brief and blazing instant, in the presence of The Rainbow, its pot of gold within my reach.

"Ah! C'est vous, Sidney?" was all he said as the door swung inward to admit me. I found myself before a man of modest stature whose dark gray hair and trim condition belied his years. Such was his composure that my coming could well have been a daily event. There followed a warm embrace, marked only by a brief heave of the shoulders, and then his voice broke slightly as he said: "At last! To have you come back into my life after all these years is unbelievable. It is a marvel! And Madame Tyler, where is she?" I raced down to the street to fetch my wife, grateful for a moment in which to recover my own composure.

With firm control of his feelings and a gracious gesture of welcome, Michel led us to a table on which stood a bottle of whiskey and three small glasses, which he promptly filled. Tensions relaxed as their warm contents brought fire to our throats. The conversation for the rest of that afternoon, and later at dinner in the home of Henri, Françoise, and their two children, was animated but inconsequential, as Michel and I, in observance of the necessary prerequisites, took the measure of each other and confirmed the mutuality which our letters had so happily promised.

The following day was spent at Aigues Mortes, that ancient walled city which was the jumping off point for the first crusades. Michel took delight in showing us the battlements and in describing the salient features of this fortified port. Perhaps he was flattered to find me an attentive pupil; and perhaps the discovery that I was content to be a willing listener who refrained from interrupting his train of thought added to his confidence. On the long drive home, almost as though we were old friends who had never been apart, he began to speak of things which he had long suppressed. Wordsworth's definition of poetry as the spontaneous expression of "emotion recollected in tranquility" came forcefully to mind as I lis-

Inspecting the ramparts at Aigues Mortes. Michel is pleased with his exposition.

tened in silence, fearful of breaking the spell which seemed to possess him.

It is strange, he mused, how your discovery of me and the correspondence which flowed between us has led me to recall things which I thought I had forgotten. Not that they came back to me easily, mind you. Many had to be dug from the back corners of my brain by efforts of will which were almost physical, and which required frequent application. I am not sure that during all these years I really wanted my memories to emerge, because many of them are painful. But your reappearance in my life has helped me to extract them, and I must tell you what I now recall.

For example, he continued, I remember nothing of the circumstances under which my father took me and my brother away during that fateful Easter week-end, nor have I any recollection of what my feelings were at the time. It is possible that I had no awareness of the significance of the event. But I do remember being on board a boat which was tossing wildly in the sea and being taken below because I was so violently seasick. I know that my physical misery was made worse by the anguish of separation from my mother, to whom I naturally turned for comfort when in distress. What ship this was and where it was going is a mystery to me. As he paused to reflect upon it, I took advantage of his silence to answer the implicit question by telling him that the TITANIC's days at sea had all been calm and that no ship of her size could be tossed about wildly except in extraordinary conditions. The vessel he remembered must therefore have been a Channel steamer en route from France to England, across a body of water notorious for its turbulence.

Michel then spoke of the long black hull with its dazzling white superstructure before which he remembered standing. It was tied to the dock, he said, and the recollection was fixed in his memory not so much because of its vast bulk looming above and beyond him, but rather because he saw it as the symbol of his permanent separation from his mother. It was the means by which, in his mind, he would be taken away from her forever, without hope of return. It filled him with sadness, and a terrible longing to be home. But he was not sure just where this view could have been. To the query in his eyes I answered that it had to be Southampton, because no docks in France at that time were big enough to accommodate a ship of the TITANIC's size. This fact, in conjunction with the inference drawn from his seasickness, convinced him that he had been taken to England and had boarded the TITANIC there, as distinct from a Cherbourg embarcation which had been earlier thought.

Chapter
Three

❧ IT WAS ON THE DAY WE SPENT IN ARLES that Michel
brought himself to speak of events on board the TITANIC.
He laughed when he acknowledged that his recollections begin
with his enjoyment of a dish of fried eggs at a table to the
side of what he remembers as a cavernous room deep inside
the ship. Why anything so unremarkable as a simple meal
in the Dining Saloon should have been fixed so firmly in his
memory is difficult to explain. One may surmise only that it
was either the first nourishment consumed by a famished boy
on being taken on board the ship, or, more likely, the last
before leaving it, in which case hunger endured in the lifeboat
might have caused him to look back with relish and with longing. Whatever the reason, the irony of initially recalling a stu-
pendous experience in terms of a very ordinary event did not
escape him.

But Michel grew serious when he talked of the night of the
sinking. He told of his terror at being awakened in the middle
of the night by a strange man in his room, and of his alarm at

Arles. Wine and cigars in the mid-day sun, and a rest for weary feet.

what the stranger and his father were doing. Perhaps, as children do, he sensed the fear that drove his father to dress the boys and get them out of their cabin with utmost speed, but he remembers no explanation being given. No doubt the sudden rupture of his peaceful sleep played its part, as did the strained expressions on the faces of those who ministered to him. It was, in effect, a living nightmare.

Michel was then moved to speak of his father's farewell message. "Do you know," he said, "that I remembered my father's exact words as he gave them to me for my mother, and that I repeated them to her without a single variation? Moreover, I retained these words in my mind until about the age of 13, when I lost the actual language but kept the substance." The boy's power of total recall over a period of nine years tells us something about the sharpness of his memory

At the Peyrou, in Montpellier, where Michel makes a point to a willing listener.

and the poignancy of the drama then taking place.

Michel told me nothing about Marcelle's reception of this message. According to the newspaper accounts of her first meeting with the press upon arrival in New York, her references to her late husband did not conceal her deep resentment. They were certainly expressed before his motive had been explained and before his valedictory had been delivered. All that Michel ever added was that the passage of time eventually brought to Marcelle the healing balm of forgiveness.

Apropos the sinking, continued Michel, there was a strange thing that I want you to know about. On the night of April 15th, which was the night the TITANIC went down, Marcelle had a vivid dream. In it, her husband entered her room and formally presented her with a letter inside a white envelope heavily bordered in black, then withdrew without saying a word. Unlike most dreams, this one remained to haunt her for many years. Its implication of mourning for her husband's death, and the extraordinary coincidence of its timing, may explain how she happened to become suspicious when she read of the survival of two fatherless French boys three days later.

My memories of the TITANIC end, concluded Michel, with the crash of the lifeboat on reaching the water. "I remember the sound of the splash, and the sensation of shock, as the little boat shivered in its attempt to right itself after its irregular descent. As to the CARPATHIA, I recall only the indignity of being hauled up the side in an ash-bucket."

Chapter Four

❦ WE CELEBRATED our last evening together by dining with Henri and Françoise and their two children at a Greek restaurant. In the relaxing warmth of a fortified wine, it was a mellow occasion and a fitting end to a visit of four days' duration. As the evening drew to a close, Henri leaned across the table and said to me: "There is something about your visit which has transformed my father. We have heard him say things to you about our family past which he rarely mentions within the privacy of our home and which he has never disclosed to an outsider. I think you have done wonders for him by enabling him to unburden himself of things long buried within him. We find him a happier person as a result of your visit, and we are all very grateful."

"I thank you for your generous words," I said in reply. "I, too, have sensed a feeling of release as our acceptance of each other grew, and I am thankful that our coming has had such happy results. If our journey to find him has helped Michel to come to terms with the past, we are the richer for having been the means of it. As for myself, I think of our whole experience as being a sort of rainbow — of space in the sense that it arches over the ocean and connects two people on different continents; and of time in the sense that two-thirds of a century are compressed and telescoped and made as though the separating years had never been, bringing our youth and later lives together. I shall always think of Michel as being the pot of gold at each base of it."

Two weeks later, we stopped briefly in Paris on our way home. I wanted to meet José Sourillan to thank him in person for his part in bringing us together, and to tell him how much the whole association meant to me. We reviewed the story, and he was astonished at the extent of the disclosures which Michel had made. "You must possess a magic key with which to unlock the doors that bound Michel for so long to silence," was what he said.

Later that evening the telephone rang. It was Sourillan, and he said: "I have just gotten back to my flat and have opened my mail. In it is a letter from Michel, and I think you might like to know what he says. He tells me that he has just had a marvelous visit from you and Mrs. Tyler; that he is deeply moved that you should have gone to so much trouble to find him; and that the re-awakening of your friendship constitutes one of the four great events of his life. I thought you would like to savor this as you fly home on the Concorde to-morrow."

Au Revoir, Michel. FORSAN ET HAEC . . . . Perhaps some day you will be glad to remember even these things.

Postscript

❧ THE FIRST DRAFT OF THIS BOOK was given to Michel during our fortnight together at St. Cast in August 1980. He reviewed the text with care, deleting some passages too sensitive to be disclosed and correcting small errors. My final version incorporated the changes he requested, and I assumed that all misstatements of fact had been eliminated when I sent him the finished product, gracefully translated into French by Mme G. Yvette Thomas. On March 6, 1981, he wrote to express his thanks and his satisfaction, and, to my surprise, he concluded by appending a short list of details in need of correction. His letter reads as follows:

"My dear Sidney:

"I was glad to receive the manuscript you sent me. I am extremely grateful. This work on which you have labored for two years contains facts concerning my family about which I was not aware. For me, they are particularly moving because they deal with the last moments of my father's life, the two

79

days that my mother spent in New York, and the weeks I spent in the United States with my late brother. I would say to you also that one of the principles to which I have always adhered, especially from the time that my research in Philosophy made me a professional in that area, has been the resolve not to forget the most important events of my past, and at the same time to preserve in my memory whatever the future might bring me on my journey through life. In my eyes, one of the most essential disciplines which Philosophy teaches is a backward view through the tunnels of time and a simultaneous receptivity to the unanticipated pathways of the future, in which one's daily encounters are enriched by unforgettable friendships. This prompts me to tell you how grateful I am for your having created this affectionate bond between us, in which Constance, too, participated by her friendly presence, and also for your, 'A Rainbow, of Time and of Space.' I add that your account will cause my children and my grandchildren to become deeply interested. The French translation you sent me will enable me to give copies to each of them; it will be easy for me to have them made here.

"Since you offer them to me so generously, I should be grateful if, when your book appears and provided you have sufficient numbers available, you would send me four copies, because several of my children and grandchildren know English.

"I began last month to draft the book on which I have been working for eight years. During these past four weeks, I have written the first 15 pages, but since the book will approximate 500 pages, I think that its completion will require another two or three years. In point of fact, it is necessary that I do the required reading at the same time that I write. I think the title will be, 'What is Knowledge?'

"I am sending you and Constance a little essay which I have just published. In it I speak of Knowledge as it is understood in the theater of Molière. Molière is one of the French authors I admire the most. Like Shakespeare, whom I also very much admire, he was both an actor and a writer.

"On two sheets of paper enclosed, I report a very small number of details of secondary importance which are not exact and which you will easily be able to correct in your English text, if it has not yet appeared and if this seems to you to be desirable.

"Thank you again, dear Sidney. I send you and Constance my warmest feelings of friendship.

Michel"

The details mentioned by Michel were indeed of secondary importance and pertained chiefly to his mother and his grandparents. He regrets my failure to state specifically that his grandmother's maiden name was Bruno; he protests that his maternal grandfather was not a woodcutter, but rather a cabinetmaker who produced fine furniture for apartments; and he asserts that his mother was born in Buenos Aires instead of Nice as I had been led to believe. He further states that it was to Genoa that Angèle returned with her baby, Marcelle, where they lived for ten years before moving to Nice in 1900. And he informs me that Marcelle was not 17 when she met her future husband, but 16, and may even have been as young as 15. Their engagement took place, he says, when she was 16.

Michel rejects my assumption that reluctant maternal consent may have been a factor in the decision of Marcelle and her fiance to elope. "To the contrary," he maintains, "I am certain that my grandmother was not opposed to the marriage of my mother."

There are other small corrections. He notes my use of the wrong pronoun in the Latin inscription on the façade of a building at Lozère. It should, he points out, have been recorded by me as "Multa renascentur *quae* jam cecidere," not "*qui* jam cecidere." Meticulous scholar that he is, Michel had quoted this correctly in his letter to me, but I had misread it. Finally, he takes exception to the phrase in which I describe his panic at the appearance of a stranger in his stateroom as being, "in effect, a living nightmare." He writes: "I did not regard it as a nightmare, because at that point I could not have believed that I would never again see my father. Rather, it was a matter of anxiety." To which I can reply only that the impression of shock he conveyed to me in describing this incident seemed amply to warrant the hyperbole.

In the only significant disagreement with my text, he disavows one sentence in which I quote certain things he said to me on the drive back from Aigues Mortes. His objection is to the lines: "I am not sure that during all these years I really wanted my memories to emerge, because many of them are painful." Consistent with the theme expressed in the body of his letter, he continues: "To the contrary, I think that beginning with my adolescence, I have always made a conscious effort not to forget even my most painful memories, and indeed even to keep them fresh within me. Moreover, these memories I retained were of my most important days. What your letters and your visit brought to me was a clearer recollection of the entire panorama of events. The memories which I had kept of this period of my life, in conjunction with your inquiries, provided me with details of events which I no longer remembered."

So be it, Michel. We may gently differ in a few of our recollections and in my interpretation of words spoken in an emotional moment; but nothing can obscure the essential truths with which your open mind and warm heart enriched us. For this, I am inexpressibly grateful.

Background

Editor's Note

The classic story of the TITANIC is one that has grabbed the imagination of thousands. This tragic mishap has had such impact that books have been written, movies made, and the story often used as the basis for fictional plots.

In January of 1912 the White Star Line issued its 1912 No. 1 Channel, showing the rates for passage on "The Largest and Finest Steamers in the World." This reference was primarily made to the two triple-screw, 66,000-tons displacement steam ships, the OLYMPIC and the mighty TITANIC. The TITANIC measured 882 feet 9 inches long and 92 feet 6 inches broad, with a registered tonnage of 45,000. Basic specifications were:

Length overall	882 ft 9 in
Length between perpendiculars	850 ft 0 in
Breadth extreme	92 ft 6 in
Depth moulded to shelter deck	64 ft 3 in
Depth moulded to bridge deck	73 ft 3 in

Total height from keel to navigation bridge	104 ft 0 in
Load draught	34 ft 6 in
Load displacement, about	52,250 tons
Block coefficient at load draught	685
Gross tonnage	46,328
IHP of reciprocating engines	30,000
Shaft HP of turbine engine	16,000

The White Star Line touted items which it felt would entice would-be passengers to book passage on "The World's Greatest Steamer." Among those items was one that appeared last on the list: "the Marconi System of Wireless Telegraphy and a Deep-Sea Signaling Apparatus installed on these steamers." This was an advancement in safety, but useful only if there were someone to receive the signal.

Among the amenities provided to tempt the public were an A La Carte Restaurant, Turkish and Electric baths, a gymnasium, a squash racquet court, a clothes pressing and cleaning room, Veranda Cafe' and Palm Court, electric heaters, lounge and reception room, reading and writing room, and the Parlor Suites.

Rates for all of these delights ranged from a low of $150.00 for the least-expensive single first class inside berth room during the winter season to $4,350.00 for a Parlor Suite with private promenade on the Promenade Deck 'B'. A Parlor Suite was comprised of a sitting room, two bedrooms—each being fitted with a wardrobe room, private bath and toilet, and a servant's room. If one needed an additional servant, a room was available for $130.00; and if four servants were berthed in a room the rate would drop to $77.50 each.

Today's comparative rates for first class accommodations on the QUEEN ELIZABETH II, from New York to Southampton, would be $2,238.00 for a single first class berth, and $16,211.25 for a Parlor Suite.

The launching of the TITANIC took place on May 31,

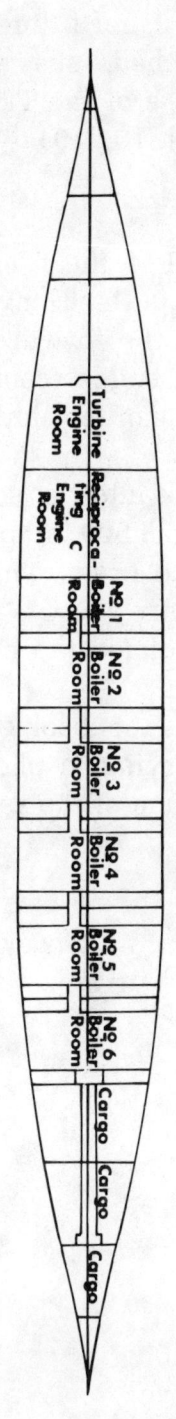

Turbine Engine Room

Reciproca- ting Engine Room

No. 1 Boiler Room

No. 2 Boiler Room

No. 3 Boiler Room

No. 4 Boiler Room

No. 5 Boiler Room

No. 6 Boiler Room

Cargo

Cargo

Cargo

Cargo

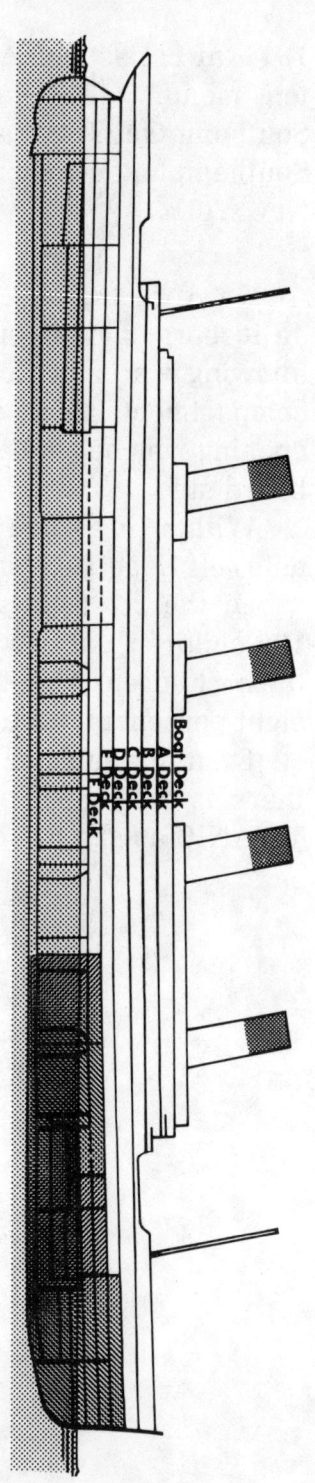

Boat Deck
A Deck
B Deck
C Deck
D Deck
E Deck
F Deck

1911, at Belfast. On April 2, 1912, her fittings completed ten months after being launched, she set sail for Southampton. The maiden voyage of the TITANIC from Southampton commenced April 10, 1912—destination New York.

On April 14, 1912, at 11:30 PM, the TITANIC struck an iceberg, slicing an opening 300 feet long in her hull, allowing water to flood five of the forward watertight compartments, including No. 5 boiler room. This huge opening was below the water line of the ship on the starboard side.

Within three hours she sank into the sea some 400 miles off Cape Race, into 2,500 to 3,500 fathoms of water.

Of the 2,206 passengers and crew, which included 105 children, only 700 people were saved—eighty-two of them children. This disaster claimed the lives of sixty-eight-percent of those on board.

Even this summer of 1981, as this book goes to press, there is a team of explorers trying to photograph the TITANIC as she lies on the bottom of the sea.

The Editors

TITANIC
Collections

TITANIC Collections go to
Philadelphia Maritime Museum

At the end of March, 1981, Charles Haas, President of the TITANIC Historical Society, Inc., announced the unanimous vote of its officers "to deposit with the Philadelphia Maritime Museum the archives, memorabilia, artifacts and library" of that Society. The transferal will take place at the end of 1981. Mr. Haas' statement of intention culminated several months of fruitful dialogues between PMM Curator Philip C. F. Smith and officers of the Society.

The TITANIC Historical Society, Inc. was founded in 1963 by a group of enthusiasts who were keen to perpetuate the memory of the "unsinkable" White Star liner, which, on April 15, 1912, during her maiden voyage, struck an iceberg 800 miles south of Newfoundland and took 1,517 people with her to the bottom.

The Society, which has more than 2,000 members worldwide, includes thirty Honorary Members who are TITANIC survivors. Videotape interviews of their recollections of that fateful night nearly seventy years ago are among the materials going to the PMM.

Since its inception, members of the TITANIC Historical Society, Inc., which publishes quarterly *The Titanic Commutator*, have been assiduous in tracking down postcards, menus, letters, fragments of carpet from First Class staterooms, manuscripts, and artifacts pertaining to the ill-fated liner. One of the largest items in the collection, its provenance carefully verified, is the life jacket which John Jacob Astor fastened to his wife shortly before he, himself, drowned.

"This is the biggest collection in the world of actual original artifacts from the TITANIC," says Louis O. Gorman, the Society's treasurer. "I think we have an obligation to future generations. I want this preserved. It's a real segment of history."

Up to now, the collections have never been available for public inspection and have been scattered in various private repositories throughout New England. The Philadelphia Maritime Museum will administer its archives, in close association with the Society, and will mount changing exhibits of the artifactual collections. For Philadelphia, connections with the TITANIC are close and varied. Several prominent citizens, including two members of the Widener family, perished in the catastrophe, and the city's own Insurance Company of North America was one of the luckless ship's various insurers.

Those people who want more information on the TITANIC may write to Mr Edward S K Kamuda, TITANIC Historical Society, P O Box 53, Indian Orchard, MA 01151.

Did you enjoy reading this AZTEX book?

May we remind you that we publish hundreds of other fine books on: aviation, boating and sailing, collecting, commercial vehicles, maritime and military subjects, model making, motorcycling, motor history and motor racing, railroads and wargaming. All our books are available through your local bookseller or, where not readily in stock, may be ordered directly from us. If you would like to be added to our catalog mailing list, and be kept regularly informed of our forthcoming and new books, please send your name and address to:

 AZTEX Corporation, P O Box 50046, Tucson, AZ 85703

94